Contents

My Country

Tuesday, 14 January

14 Huron Drive
Toronto
Ontario
Canada M3C 9S7

Dear Alex,

Hi! *Bonjour!* (You say 'bon-jor'.) In Canada we speak English and French.

My name is Hayley Cable and I'm 8 years old. I live with my family in Toronto, the biggest city in Canada. I have a sister, Stephanie, who is 6 and a brother, Scott, who is 2.

I can't wait to help you with your school project on Canada.

From

Hayley ↗

Here I am with my family. I'm in front, on the left next to Stephanie. At the back, from left to right are Dad, Scott and Mum.

Andy **hard**

CHERRYTREE BOOKS

Titles in this series

AUSTRALIA · BANGLADESH · BRAZIL · CANADA · CHINA · COSTA RICA · EGYPT · FRANCE · GERMANY · GREECE · INDIA · INDONESIA · IRELAND · ITALY · JAMAICA · JAPAN · KENYA · MEXICO · NIGERIA · PAKISTAN · POLAND · RUSSIA · SAUDI ARABIA · SOUTH AFRICA · SPAIN · SWEDEN · THE USA

A Cherrytree Book

Conceived and produced by

Nutshell
MEDIA

www.nutshellmedialtd.co.uk

First published in paperback in 2009 by
Evans Brothers Ltd
2A Portman Mansions
Chiltern Street
London W1U 6NR

© Copyright Evans Brothers 2004

Editor: Katie Orchard
Design: Mayer Media Ltd
Map artwork: Encompass Graphics Ltd
All other artwork: Mayer Media Ltd

All photographs were taken by Chris Fairclough,
except p23: Michael Dent; p24 (top), p27 (bottom), p28
(top): Government of Canada; p27 (top): Heidi Kaulbach.

Acknowledgements
The authors would like to thank the following for their
help: the Cable family; the headmistress, staff and pupils
of The Rosedale Day School, Toronto.

British Library Cataloguing in Publication Data
Orchard, Andy
  Canada. – (Letters from around the world)
  1. Canada – Social conditions – 1991 – – Juvenile
  literature
  2. Canada – Social life and customs – 1945 – – Juvenile
  literature
  I. Title II. Orchard, Clare
  971' . 0648

ISBN 978-1842345641

Printed in China by WKT Co. Ltd.

Cover: Hayley (centre) with Lian (left) and Olivia (right),
on a ferry on Lake Ontario.
Title page: Hayley and some of her friends.
This page: A view of the CN Tower and Toronto skyline.
Contents page: Hayley and Julia paint Easter eggs.
Glossary page: Hayley and Stephanie scooter to school.
Further information page: An Inuit art lesson.
Index: A game of street hockey outside Hayley's house.

In the past, people came from France and Britain to settle in Canada. Today, French and English are the two official languages.

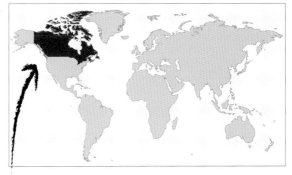

Canada's place in the world.

Canada is the second-largest country in the world, after Russia. It can take more than two weeks to drive from one side to the other.

0   200   400   600   800 kilometres

0   200   400 miles

N

ARCTIC OCEAN

GREENLAND (Denmark)

Alaska (USA)

Baffin Bay

Baffin Island

Mackenzie

Mount Logan 5,959m

YUKON TERRITORY

Great Bear Lake

NORTHWEST TERRITORIES

NUNAVUT

ATLANTIC OCEAN

PACIFIC OCEAN

ROCKY MOUNTAINS

BRITISH COLUMBIA

Great Slave Lake

C A N A D A

Hudson Bay

NEWFOUNDLAND & LABRADOR

ALBERTA

SASKATCHEWAN

Edmonton

MANITOBA

St John's

QUEBEC

Calgary

Vancouver

Lake Winnipeg

PRINCE EDWARD ISLAND

Saskatoon

ONTARIO

NEW BRUNSWICK

Charlottetown

Regina

Winnipeg

Lake Superior

St Lawrence

NOVA SCOTIA

Morris

OTTAWA

Quebec City

Halifax

UNITED STATES OF AMERICA

Lake Huron

Montreal

Fredericton

Lake Michigan

Toronto

Lake Ontario

Niagara Falls

Lake Erie

Canada is divided up into ten provinces and three territories. Toronto is in the province of Ontario, on the eastern side of Canada.

Toronto is beside Lake Ontario. This is one of five large lakes along the border between Canada and the USA, known as the Great Lakes.

Toronto's skyscrapers tower over Lake Ontario. The tall building on the left is the Canadian National (CN) Tower, which is 533 metres high.

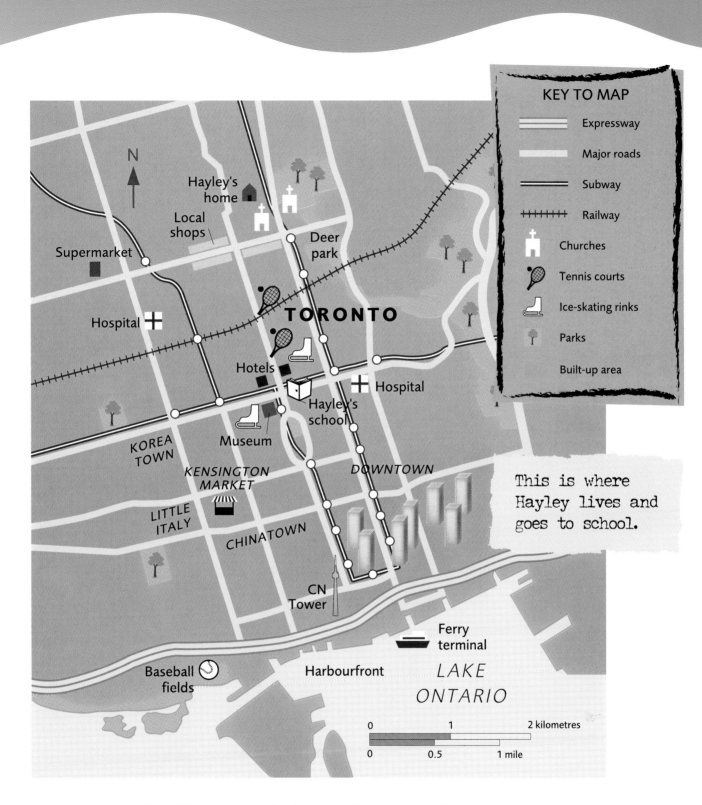

KEY TO MAP

- Expressway
- Major roads
- Subway
- ++++++++ Railway
- Churches
- Tennis courts
- Ice-skating rinks
- Parks
- Built-up area

Hayley's home

Local shops

Supermarket

Deer park

Hospital

TORONTO

Hotels

Hospital

Hayley's school

Museum

KOREA TOWN

KENSINGTON MARKET

LITTLE ITALY

CHINATOWN

DOWNTOWN

CN Tower

Ferry terminal

Baseball fields

Harbourfront

LAKE ONTARIO

This is where Hayley lives and goes to school.

| 0 | | 1 | | 2 kilometres |
| 0 | 0.5 | | 1 mile | |

More than 5 million people live in Toronto. People go from all over the world to live and work there. The city is full of shops, offices and restaurants, with signs in many languages.

Landscape and Weather

Canada has many large forests and lakes. In the west, there is a big mountain range called the Rocky Mountains, which stretches south into the USA. In the middle of Canada there are great plains called 'prairies', where there are many farms.

The Rocky Mountains and their lakes are very popular places for climbing, hiking, skiing and canoeing.

Some parts of northern Canada are covered in snow and ice all year round. The warmest part of Canada is along the border with the USA. Toronto is warmer than most of Canada. It has snowy winters and very hot summers.

Snowshoes were invented by the Native Canadians to stop their feet sinking into soft snow.

Toronto's Climate

January

Temperature

-5°C

23mm

Rainfall

July

Temperature

22°C

71mm

Rainfall

At Home

Hayley's family lives on a quiet street, very near the city centre, not far from Lake Ontario. There is a busy street close by with lots of shops and a subway station.

Hayley's family lives in a three-storey house. The house is 80 years old. It used to belong to Hayley's grandfather.

Hayley's quiet street is perfect for playing street hockey. One of the players always looks out for traffic.

Hayley's house has a gas fire, central heating and double glazing to keep it warm in the winter. During the hot summer, the windows have net screens to keep out biting insects, such as mosquitoes.

Hayley's family and a friend keep warm by the gas fire in the living room.

Downstairs there is a kitchen, a dining room and a living room. Upstairs are the bedrooms, bathrooms and a study.

Hayley shares a bedroom with her sister, Stephanie, on the third floor.

Hayley helps
her mum unload
the dishwasher
at the weekend.

During the long, cold
winter there are no
flowers in the yard.

Like most homes in Canada, Hayley's house has a large fridge, cooker and dishwasher.

After the snow has melted, the family spends more time outside. In the summer, they have barbecues on a wooden balcony called the deck. Down the steps from the deck is the back garden, called the yard.

Wednesday, 5 February

14 Huron Drive
Toronto
Ontario
Canada M3C 9S7

Dear Alex,

Thanks for your letter. I liked reading about your friends.
Do you ever have sleepovers? They're really popular over
here. We often have them at weekends. My friend, Heather,
came to my house for a sleepover last Friday after school.
We did our homework together, had dinner and then played
until bedtime. We even had a pillow-fight!

From

Hayley

Mum put an extra
mattress on the
floor for Heather
to sleep on.

Food and Mealtimes

On schooldays, Hayley has cereal, fruit and a glass of milk for breakfast. She usually has a packed lunch of sandwiches, yoghurt, carrot or celery sticks and a blueberry muffin.

At the weekend, many Canadian families have 'brunch' – a mixture of breakfast and lunch.

For brunch at weekends, Hayley and her family usually have bacon and eggs, followed by pancakes and maple syrup.

There are many different types of food for sale in Toronto. As well as food produced in Canada, such as beef and maple syrup, there are also shops selling food from all around the world.

Hayley's mother buys fresh fruit and vegetables from a street stall in China Town.

Hayley's favourite meal is Italian pizza.

On many weekends,
Hayley's grandparents
come to her house for
a family meal.

Family gatherings often
involve a special dinner.
Each year in October,
Canadians have a very
special meal, called
Thanksgiving. This usually
includes roast turkey and
pumpkin pie.

There is a huge choice of take-
away restaurants in Toronto,
including Chinese, Indian,
Korean and Thai. Hayley loves
eating Greek kebabs.

Thursday, 27 February

14 Huron Drive
Toronto
Ontario
Canada M3C 9S7

Dear Alex,

My dad makes great pancakes, just like the ones you have on Shrove Tuesday! This is his recipe:

You will need: 375ml milk, 40g melted butter, 350g flour, 1 egg, 1 tablespoon baking powder, 1 tablespoon sugar, pinch of salt.

1. Mix the flour, salt, baking powder and sugar in a bowl.
2. In another bowl beat together the egg, milk and butter.
3. Stir both mixtures together to make a smooth 'batter'.
4. Grease and heat a pan. Add 2 tablespoons of batter and spread it thinly over the bottom of the pan. When it is brown on one side, flip it over to cook the other side. (Dad always does that bit for me.)

They're great with maple syrup!

From
Hayley

I always mix the batter for the pancakes.

School Day

Hayley's school is not far from her home. Most children travel there by car, by bus or on foot. School starts at 8.30 a.m. and finishes at 3 p.m.

Hayley and Stephanie set off for school on their scooters. They always wear safety helmets.

Hayley's teacher has written the names of all Hayley's lessons on the board in French.

Hayley has lessons in maths, history, science, geography, music, English, gym (which is like P.E.) and French. English and French are the two official languages of Canada. Most people speak mainly English. In the province of Quebec, people speak mainly French.

At Hayley's school, the older children help the younger ones learn to read. They are called 'reading buddies'.

Hayley reads a story with two younger children.

Hayley works on an art project about the Inuit people. The Inuit were some of the first people to live in Canada.

Most Canadian children start school at the age of 6. This is called Grade 1. Most of them finish school in Grade 12, when they are 17.

Hayley's classmates play soccer on the school playing field.

Thursday, 20 March

14 Huron Drive
Toronto
Ontario
Canada M3C 9S7

Dear Alex,

Hi buddy! (In Canada we call our friends buddies or buds.)
I'm glad you liked the pancakes.

What do you like doing at school? I like art. I have joined an art
and crafts club. Today we drew Inuit masks. The Inuit people,
one of the 'First Nations', have lived in Canada for many
hundreds of years.

My other favourite subject is gym. We're learning to play soccer
just now. You call it 'football', but that's a different game over
here. How confusing!

From
Hayley

Here are some
of my buds from
class with Carrie,
our gym teacher.

Off to Work

Hayley's mum is an estate agent. She helps people buy and sell their homes. In a big city like Toronto, there are lots of estate agents.

Hayley's dad works for a large company selling books over the Internet.

Hayley's mum puts up a 'For Sale' sign.

Streetcars run on rails in the road. They are powered by cables that run overhead.

Nearly 3 million people work in Toronto's busy shops, offices and factories. They travel to work from all over the city by car, train, bus and streetcar.

Outside the city there are large farms, where animals such as beef cattle are raised and crops such as wheat are grown.

Logging is an important industry in Canada. At timber mills like this one, logs are made into paper, plywood and wood pulp.

Free Time

In Canada, people love sport. They play ice hockey, lacrosse, baseball, basketball and Canadian football. Soccer is becoming very popular. In the winter many people go skiing in the Rocky Mountains. In the summer, families visit the national parks and lakes all over Canada.

Canadian football is very similar to American football, but the pitch is longer and wider.

In the winter, Hayley goes ice-skating with her friends.

Monday, 7 April

14 Huron Drive
Toronto
Ontario
Canada M3C 9S7

Dear Alex,

Street hockey is very popular in Canada. Yesterday we watched the Street Hockey Jamboree – it was really exciting! Once a year, teams from all over Toronto get together to play hockey in the main street. The street is closed to traffic for the whole day.

Lots of people wear blue and white. These are the colours of Toronto's hockey team, the Maple Leafs. Our Toronto baseball team is called the Blue Jays. They wear blue and white, too!

From

Hayley

It was cold watching the street hockey in the snow!

Religion and Special Days

Most Canadians are Christians. Others are Jewish, Muslim, Hindu, Sikh or Buddhist. There are churches, mosques, synagogues and temples all over Toronto.

Hayley's family celebrates the Christian festivals of Christmas and Easter.

Hayley and her friend, Julia, have painted these eggs for Easter.

A person prays in a Buddhist temple in Toronto.

People celebrate other special days, too. Canada Day is on 1 July. It celebrates the naming of Canada in 1867. Rodeo stampedes are popular summer festivals in Canada. The most famous one is the Calgary Stampede. There is a rodeo, wagon racing and dancing.

Wagons race to the finish at the Morris Stampede. Morris has the second-largest rodeo, after Calgary.

Fact File

Capital city: The capital of Canada is Ottawa. It has a population of 1 million.

Other major cities: Toronto, Montreal, Vancouver, Calgary, Edmonton, Quebec City and Winnipeg.

Size: 9,971,500km^2

Population: 33.2 million. This is not many people for such a large country.

Languages: English and French.

Flag: The Canadian flag is red and white. These colours are also in the English and French flags. It has a red maple leaf in the middle. The maple leaf flag was first raised on 15 February, 1965.

Currency: Dollar (divided into cents). 1 dollar = 100 cents. A dollar coin is called a 'loonie', because it has a picture of a bird called a loon on it. A two-dollar coin is called a 'toonie'.

Stamps: Canadian stamps often show sports or animals. These stamps show a hockey player, a polar bear and a beaver. The beaver is the national animal of Canada.

Main religions: There are many Catholics and Protestants in Canada. There are also Muslims, Hindus, Buddhists, Sikhs and Jews.

Main industries: Canada's main industries are wheat farming, logging, asbestos production, and nickel, silver and zinc mining.

Mounties: Canada is famous for its mounted police, who ride specially trained horses and wear red tunics and large hats.

Niagara Falls: Canada's most famous landmarks are the Niagara Falls. These are two very large waterfalls on the border of the USA and Canada. The Canadian Falls are 54m high and 640m wide. The US Falls are just over 55m high and 328m wide.

Highest point: Mount Logan (5,959m). Several peaks in the Canadian Rocky Mountains rise above 3,000m.

Longest river: The Mackenzie River in the north is 4,241km long.

History: Vikings from northern Europe came to Canada about 1,000 years ago, and briefly settled there. Most settlers came from Britain and France, 500 years later. Native Canadian people lived there long before the Europeans arrived. The name 'Canada' comes from a Native Canadian word for 'village'.

Glossary

Canadian football A sport very similar to American football, but played on a different-sized pitch.

First Nations The first people to live in Canada, before Europeans arrived and settled there.

Great Lakes The group of five large lakes along the border between Canada and the USA. Four of the Great Lakes have shores in both countries.

hockey A sport played on ice, and known outside Canada as ice hockey. Hockey played on grass is called field hockey. It is also played in the streets and is called street hockey.

Inuit One of the First Nations, who have traditionally lived in the northern part of Canada.

lacrosse The national sport of Canada, played with a ball and a stick with a net at the end.

Native Canadians Another name for the First Nations.

province An area within Canada that is like a 'mini-country'.

rodeo stampede A festival of cowboy activities. The most famous one takes place in Calgary once a year.

streetcar Buses that run on rails through city streets like trains, powered by an overhead cable.

territories Three large areas in Canada that do not have many big cities. The three territories are called the Northwest Territories, Nunavut and Yukon Territory.

Further Information

Information books:

All About Continents: North and South America by Bruce McClish (Heinemann, 2003)

Countries of the World: Canada by Sally Garrington (Evans Brothers Ltd, 2005)

The Changing Face of Canada by Catherine Little (Hodder Wayland, 2002)

What's it Like to Live in Canada? by Catherine Little (Hodder Wayland, 2003)

Fiction:

Anne of Green Gables by Lucy Maud Montgomery (Penguin Readers, 2002)

Websites:

The Canadian Government
http://canada.gc.ca/
Facts, figures, photographs and maps with many useful links.

CIA World Factbook
https://www.cia.gov/library/
publications/the-world-factbook/
Facts and figures about Canada
and other countries.

Gander Academy's Canadian Resources on the WWW
http://www.stemnet.nf.ca/CITE/
canada.htm
A site designed for kids, including resources for teachers.

Canadian Tourism Commission
www.travelcanada.ca/
Includes a virtual tour of Canada, with photographs from all over the country.

Index